In grateful memory of Jella Lepman, who has given me not only her story, through *A Bridge of Children's Books*, but also many friends around the world, through IBBY and the writing of this book, including especially my now-cherished friend and Jella's granddaughter, Claudia Lepman Logan. —K. P.

For my family and friends: Thank you for always listening to me ramble on and on about my favorite books. —S. D.

Library of Congress Cataloging-in-Publication Data available.

ISBN 978-1-4521-8262-9

Manufactured in China.

Design by Sara Gillingham Studio.
Typeset in Archer.
The illustrations in this book were rendered in pencil and colored digitally.

10 9 8 7 6 5 4 3 2 1

Chronicle books and gifts are available at special quantity discounts to corporations, professional associations, literacy programs, and other organizations. For details and discount information, please contact our premiums department at corporatesales@chroniclebooks.com or at 1-800-759-0190.

Handprint Books
An imprint of Chronicle Books LLC
680 Second Street
San Francisco, California 94107

Chronicle Books—we see things differently.
Become part of our community at www.chroniclekids.com.

Jella Lepman

and Her Library of Dreams

The Woman Who Rescued a Generation of Children and
Founded the World's Largest Children's Library

KATHERINE PATERSON
and Jella helped —K.P.

Illustrated by SALLY DENG

HANDPRINT BOOKS

AN IMPRINT OF CHRONICLE BOOKS · SAN FRANCISCO

Everything about the flight was miserable. Of course, it wasn't meant to be comfortable. The man and woman were on a military transport built during World War II to ferry troops and armaments to the front. On this trip from England to Germany in 1945, the American colonel was crammed into his bucket seat along one side of the plane, facing across the cargo space toward a row of passenger seats on the other side. There was no looking out any of the few windows, and the exit doors were meant for paratroopers to leap from.

But there he sat, next to a middle-aged woman in an ill-fitting uniform with the golden oak leaf of a major pinned to her shoulder. What in the world was a woman doing on this plane? The Allies had defeated Germany. Its cities had been bombed to rubble, but the war was hardly over. Nazism was not dead. The army needed men, not women, to maintain order in the occupied zone.

The noise of the engines made conversation nearly impossible. Still, there were the two of them, strapped side by side, so he tried:

"If you were reincarnated, what would you rather be, a man or a woman?"

"Assuming that's a purely hypothetical question," she said, in the high-pitched, snooty voice of the European elite, "probably neither. I'd like to be a titmouse or a sunflower."

That might have ended the conversation right there, but the colonel was curious about this strange woman. Her accent revealed that she was definitely not an American, so what was she doing posing as a major in the American army? Curiosity won the day. He blurted out his real question: "Just why are you in uniform? What does headquarters want you to do? Can you tell me?"

"Reeducation, Colonel, or that's the way they put it. I'm supposed to work with women and children. That's all I know at the moment and, probably, all headquarters at Bad Homburg knows. Maybe somebody imagined that an undertaking such as this needed the feminine touch."

A few bumps and loops of the plane ended the conversation. The woman closed her eyes, probably fighting air sickness. *Women are such weak creatures*, the colonel thought.

Perhaps the colonel would have been amazed to know that Jella Lepman, for that was the woman's name, was also asking herself why she was in the uniform of an American officer, flying from London back to the land from which she, as a Jew, had fled nine years before.

Although Jella said very little about her early life, even to her children and grandchildren, some parts of the story are known. Her life began on May 15, 1891, in the German city of Stuttgart, where she was born into a Jewish family, the eldest of the three daughters of Josef and Flora Lehmann. It was a comfortable life. Josef Lehmann owned a men's clothing store. His daughters attended an elite academy, established nearly a hundred years earlier by Queen Katharina "for the daughters of the educated classes." Here, among other academic studies, Jella was taught French, English, and music. After graduation she spent a year at a boarding school near Lausanne, Switzerland.

By the time she returned to Stuttgart, Jella was an accomplished young musician and had dreams of becoming a concert pianist, but Papa forbade it. And although her parents might have been liberal in religion and politics, in the home, Papa's word was law. Her other great passion was books, and this love, rather than music, was to become her life's work.

So the 17-year-old Jella did a most unusual thing for a girl who had been raised in comfort and educated abroad: She opened a reading room with books in several languages for the children of the immigrant workers who had come to Stuttgart to work in the tobacco factory there. This may have been her first close encounter with children far less fortunate than her young self, but it proved to be the start of a life spent working with children who suffered privation and dislocation. She could not have known that her own daughter and son would be among them.

Gustav Lepman was 14 years older than she, but that didn't stop Jella from marrying him in 1913. Gustav lived in the nearby town of Feuerbach. His German American parents had come to Germany to be part owners of a duvet factory there. Jella and Gustav had only been married a couple of years when war came. Although his parents were American citizens, he had been born in Germany and was drafted to serve in the German army during World War I.

Jella and Gustav's daughter, Anne-Marie, was born in 1918 and their son, Gunther, in 1921.

But war had left its terrible marks on Gustav's body and spirit. In 1922, at the age of 45, he died of a heart attack. He left what should have been a generous insurance policy of 100,000 Reichsmarks, which in 1918 would have been roughly a half million American dollars, but when he died, Germany was suffering from runaway inflation. The insurance money Jella actually received was not enough to buy a rosebush for her husband's grave.

It was the first time in her life that Jella faced poverty. What was a penniless 31-year-old widow with two tiny children to do? Her father had died before she was married, so she could not expect help from her family. She had always loved words, so she turned to a career as a writer. She worked as a journalist and columnist and, amazingly enough, became the first woman editor of the liberal newspaper *Stuttgarter Neues Tagblatt* (New Daily Paper).

The 16-story Tagblatt Tower was the tallest building in the city. It was lit on the outside at night, it was said, so that the citizens of Stuttgart, seeing the light, would realize that their own ordinary lives were worth living and worth reporting upon.

Jella wrote about women's issues and books for children. She was very active in politics as a member of the German Democratic Party, and she became a leader in its women's section. In 1929 Jella ran for a seat in the Reichstag, or parliament, a brave act for a woman of that time.

And it was a terrible time. The nation had never recovered from the wounds of World War I. Germany was in chaos, both economically and politically. The despair of the people made possible the rise of a demagogue who played on their fears of Russian communism and blamed their economic woes on the Jewish people. In the election of 1930, the one in which Jella lost her bid, the National Socialist Party, or the Nazi Party, gained twice as many legislative seats as it had in the previous election. The worldwide depression only made life more miserable for the German people, and the appeal of Nazi leader Adolf Hitler was growing. He promised law and order and the abolition of the communists and the Jewish people. In short, Hitler promised to make Germany great again.

In 1933, to the cheers of the crowds and with the assent of the industrialists, Hitler seized total control of the German government.

Jella Lepman, one of the Nazis' despised Jewish people, lost her job. The next year, 1934, Hitler abolished freedom of the press. The previously liberal *Tagblatt* became a tool for Nazi propaganda. Needing to support her family, Jella worked as a freelancer until friends convinced her that she had to leave her homeland entirely. In 1936 Jella and her two teenage children fled to Italy, where a kind widow gave them temporary shelter. But Benito Mussolini, Italy's strongman, was becoming more like Hitler every day, so Jella knew the family had to run again. An Italian friend found a job in England for 19-year-old Anne-Marie. She was to teach conversational German in a boarding school. Soon after Anne-Marie left, a place was found in a Bournemouth boarding school for Gunther.

Jella and her son left Italy for England. She wrote about these years: "Words cannot express the pain of emigration, the powerlessness to save the children from such suffering. They will never be able to forget it. England and its boarding schools were a wonderful help, freedom something precious."

Although she had found safety for her children, once again she herself was stateless and jobless. She later said of that time, "The map of London imprinted on the soles of my boots, occasionally finding meager breadwinning work."

Her first real job came from another refugee from Hitler's Germany. Olga Schnitzler, the ex-wife of the prominent Austrian Jewish novelist and playwright Arthur Schnitzler, had somehow managed to save the author's literary papers from Nazi destruction and brought them to England. They needed a proper sorting out. Olga Schnitzler knew Jella and suggested that she should be given the task of reviewing and cataloging the papers. Meanwhile, Jella's proficiency in English, her third language, was rapidly improving.

In London Jella's talents as journalist and editor eventually were valued. She worked for both the British Broadcasting Corporation (BBC) and the American Broadcasting Station in Europe. She also wrote a book entitled *Women in Nazi Germany*. In it she told how Hitler's lies had been embraced by ordinary housewives whose lives were a struggle for economic security and simple human dignity, and how none of his promises to women had been kept. The lives of women in Germany were a subject on which she was an expert, but she published under the pseudonym Katherine Thomas and fictionalized details about the journalist narrator. Using her own name and experience would have endangered anyone back in Germany known to have associated with her.

Jella and her children lived through what was perhaps the most harrowing time in England's history, the days and years when it seemed inevitable that the Germans would bomb London to oblivion and invade the country.

After what British prime minister Winston Churchill called Britain's "darkest hour," the 1941 bombing of Pearl Harbor, Hawaii, pushed the United States into what was now a world war. It became a leader of the Allied forces alongside Britain, the Soviet Union, and later China. With the Allies' invasion of Normandy, France, in 1944, the tide slowly turned, and the Allied forces began to win.

By the end of April 1945, when Hitler knew that the Russians had Berlin surrounded and that the Americans had cut off any escape routes, he died by suicide. On May 8, Churchill declared that the war in Europe was over.

The Allies did not want a repeat of the events that had followed Germany's defeat in World War I. Jella's talents were now turned to the effort to bring normalcy to a devastated Europe. She and a team of international journalists, including women who edited American fashion magazines, were charged with the task of publishing a magazine that was called *Frau und Welt* (Women and World). The magazine would be published in a number of European languages and distributed all over Europe, including in those countries that had joined Germany and Italy to fight the Allies.

Jella greatly enjoyed this experience. It was important work in a congenial atmosphere, so the appearance of an American colonel asking her to take on a different assignment was not necessarily welcomed.

The colonel wanted her to go back to Germany as soon as possible to be an "adviser on the cultural and educational needs of women and children" in an area now occupied by the American and other Allied forces.

Jella was shaken by this request. She had lived under the Nazi regime. She knew what had happened then and the even more terrible things that had occurred since she fled. How could she ever return?

Her friends were no help. They gave contradictory advice. An American editor even said she was envious of Jella: "You have the education, you know the language, and you've lived with these people. I, now, could never fill such a post. I'd be utterly foreign in it." Or perhaps too frightened?

Others urged her not to go: "Do you believe the Nazi spirit is really dead? It will last for generations, even with the best help in the world. German bombs might have killed you at any time in the last six years. Isn't that enough for you?" Her friend Anna Freud, daughter of the famous Sigmund Freud, the founder of psychoanalysis, counseled, "You've already suffered too much. At last you're beginning to put down roots here, and anyway, you know people can't be reeducated."

As Jella debated, she remembered a scene from just before Britain went to war.

Jewish children from the countries the Nazis had occupied were being allowed to enter England. The daughter of one of Jella's German friends was among them. At the time, Jella felt unable to take in the girl herself, but arrangements had been made for a family in Leeds to care for her. Jella went to the train station to meet the child, part of a group of about 50 in this Kindertransport (child transport). The girl silently ate a bowl of soup in the station waiting room but didn't even pick up the precious orange on the plate beside her. Loving Jewish parents, fearing for what would happen next under the Nazis, had sent these children to a safer place. But for the children, it meant loneliness and confusion in a strange land with an unknown language. They may not have realized that they would probably never see their parents again, but they certainly knew that something terrible was happening.

Even if Jella could not help the adults, couldn't she do something for suffering children? "I found it easy to believe that the children all too soon would fall into the wrong hands if no help came from the world outside," she wrote. "Were not

Germany's children just as innocent as children all over the world, helpless victims of monstrous events?"

    She had made up her mind. The fate of these children was too important. She would accept the military assignment.

The transport plane landed at last in Frankfurt, and a car was waiting to take
Jella and a young Canadian woman on to the American headquarters in Bad
Homburg. The Frankfurt they drove through was not the elegant city that
Jella had known as a child. It was nothing but rubble and shadowy people
creeping in and out of the ruins, not looking up, even at the sound of a large
American car. But on that strange journey, Jella later remembered the sight
of a child holding an autumn flower who smiled and waved as they passed.

When they arrived in Bad Homburg at a house marked "Quartermaster," their papers were examined. The Canadian woman was sent one direction and Jella another. The officer on duty looked at Jella's military orders and then grabbed a phone: "Colonel, what should I do? There is a *female* here with the rank of a major. Where am I supposed to put her up for the night?"

It was a strange couple of days for Jella. She slept on the floor wrapped in two scratchy wool blankets, while in the officers' mess was a feast, with wonderful food from America and wine from France. But Jella's stomach was accustomed to the sparse wartime rations of England. It turned at the sight of the almost obscene bounty spread out before her.

Jella's first inkling of what her assignment was to be came during a meeting of the information control staff in the colonel's office. The staff's job was to sort out the "good" Germans from the "bad" and work with the good ones to carry out a program of cultural reconstruction in the American zone. She quickly got the idea that the colonel was sure there were competent, right-thinking Germans, and with proper reeducation, a new society (mostly along the lines of an idealized American society) would rise from the ashes of the defeated and devastated enemy. Jella, being the only female present, would be responsible for German women and children. What kind of aid would be needed to carry out this goal on their behalf?

It was a next-to-impossible assignment, and Jella realized at once that she would not accomplish anything sitting behind a desk at headquarters in Bad Homburg.

She made her way to the general's office and found in General Robert A. McClure a man of intelligence, lacking the arrogance of many of the officers she had met—a man willing to listen to a "mere" female. The general agreed that she needed to make a fact-finding journey through the Allied occupation zone. For how was she to know what was needed unless she saw it for herself? General McClure not only gave her permission for the tour but also provided a jeep and a driver.

Jella compared her jeep to a magic horse that could safely fly over potholes and bomb craters and never conk out. Her American driver was less than magical. He seemed to have no sense of direction, couldn't read a map, and cursed liberally. Fortunately, Jella couldn't understand most of the obscenities. But she grew very fond of the man who uttered them. Even if Joe didn't know east from west, how could she resist caring for a young man who'd never left his home in the Midwest until he was thrust into the invasion? A boy who showed her pictures of his family and spoke

longingly of the sweetheart waiting for him—who drew red crosses on the calendar, counting the days until he could return home?

Jella and Joe's first destination was Heidelberg, the ancient and beautiful university city on the banks of the Neckar River. It was the German city least damaged in the war, so it was crowded with refugees. Her first stop was at the home of her old friend Professor Alfred Weber, a world-renowned sociologist and political scientist who had been an early and vocal opponent of the rise of Nazism. When Hitler took power in 1933, Professor Weber resigned his position at the university in protest.

Jella found him living in the attic of what had been his home. The rest of the house was now filled with refugees. Paper was pasted over the broken windows in an attempt to keep out the autumn chill. Jella saw her friend now old and bone thin, perhaps as broken as his window glass.

He refused to take the hand she held out to him. "No," he said. "I cannot take your hand. Germany has brought too much horror and misery upon the world, and I too am guilty." Jella was deeply moved. Here was a man who had risked everything to oppose Hitler, yet he took upon himself the sins of his nation. His immediate concern was not for himself but for the homeless. What would happen to them with winter fast approaching?

When Jella and Joe finally arrived in Stuttgart, where so many of the buildings had been destroyed, Joe looked at the ruins and through his chewing-gum-filled mouth muttered, "What a hole." Of course, he had no way of knowing that Jella had been born in Stuttgart and spent most of her life in this once-prosperous city. Joe asked a policeman for directions to the headquarters of the military government and was pointed to one of the few undamaged structures—the Tagblatt Tower. Seeing her old workplace made Jella tremble so hard she could barely make herself get out of the jeep.

Imagine Joe's surprise when the tower's porter rushed out of a cubicle and began to wave madly at his passenger. "You're back again," he cried. "Wonderful! Now everything will be all right."

What a performance! Jella thought. In her mind she could see the porter greeting everyone who had come to the door for the last 12 years with an upraised arm and the words "Heil Hitler!"

Soon the whole German workforce was pouring out of the building to see her. All of them were saying something like, "You're back! Now everything will be all right again." Unlike Professor Weber, these people had kept their jobs. They had survived by submitting to the Nazi authority and publishing the propaganda of the regime, and now they were simply dismissing the horrors of the past, thinking it would be easy to just go back to the way things were before the Nazis had taken possession of the paper and fired their Jewish editor.

Jella felt like a stranger in the midst of a crowd of strangers. *But perhaps that is what frail human beings are like,* she thought. Despite the hell of the Holocaust, the decimation of cities, the deaths of millions, the near destruction of civilization itself, most of the survivors simply wanted everything to go back and be just as it was before.

The suffering of the children was everywhere apparent. Whenever the jeep stopped, ragged, hungry urchins would surround it and beg, sometimes in the broken English they had picked up from American soldiers.

When Jella would ask them about their parents and where their homes were, it was clear they had no homes. Without any show of feeling, they would say their parents were dead or wandering some road, or actually they didn't know where. In the same unemotional way, they told her of what they had seen in their short lives—murders, hangings, robberies, and crimes too awful for her to repeat. But Jella thought she saw in the eyes of these children something still childlike. It astonished her and gave her hope.

For their own protection many of the homeless children formed into gangs and lived together as makeshift families in the ruins. There were child "parents" who organized scrounging for fuel, making fires, and cooking what scraps they could forage. Little eight-year-old "mothers" dressed and cleaned and cared for younger brothers and sisters.

But not all the gangs were run by loving elder siblings. Jella told of one pretty little girl who was lovely to look at even in her rags. She had violet eyes and curls that fell to her shoulders. She was so appealing that even without begging, she was showered with treats by the soldiers coming out of the PX, or post exchange, the shop

where American servicepeople bought their goods and groceries. One day Jella decided to follow her to see where she lived. The girl disappeared into a bombed-out building. Jella cautiously peered in. Waiting for the child were two large boys who emptied her apron full of goodies into a big bag and raced away, leaving her crying and alone. Jella went in the doorway and asked gently, "Can I do anything for you?" The child looked up, her eyes full of suspicion, and immediately disappeared.

A social worker explained the system to Jella. The little girl was one of many waifs who were trained to lure food and gifts for the benefit of the gangs. They taught her how to get goods and then took them from her to sell on the black market. At the end of the day she might be given something to keep her alive and useful. However cruelly the gang members treated her, she would never dare disobey them.

It was obvious that the children of Germany whom Jella had come home to help were in desperate need of food, of clothing, of safe shelter. Elly Heuss-Knapp, whose husband later became president of West Germany, told Jella that while soup kitchens and care packages were all good and necessary, "nourishment for the soul" was even more important.

For Jella that nourishment had always come from books. She began to talk to publishers and booksellers. One bookseller told her that the people were hungry for the books from the free world that had been banned for 12 years.

"And children's books?" Jella asked.

"Children's books? Oh, there aren't any of those left whatsoever. Those are more needed than all the others."

But when she talked to publishers about translating and publishing books for German children, all they would consider were books like *Robinson Crusoe*, *Gulliver's Travels*, and *Uncle Tom's Cabin*. They seemed to think that if they republished these old classics, it would please their occupiers. Jella wasn't interested in pleasing American or British generals; she wanted to please children. What about the classics of German children's literature that had been outlawed and burned in the Nazi era? Or what about the current books being published in other countries? Perhaps if they saw modern books from abroad, German publishers would be interested. Jella would have to figure out a way to make that happen. She had done all the fact-finding she needed to do. The time for action had come.

Once again, Jella was to be the only woman in a room full of men, headed by General McClure. The fact that she was a major among other senior officers didn't matter. She was still a "mere" female. She was there to report on her fact-finding journey, and she could be quite sure that they would not understand her conclusions. There was no way to combine all the women and children of Germany into a single lump, she told them. But there was one thing they all needed—something "to hold on to," to nourish the soul. The officers listened politely, but they must have been startled by the solution Jella proposed: She thought one way to give them this nourishment was to arrange an exhibition of the best children's books from around the world. "Bit by bit, let us set this upside-down world right again by starting with the children. They will show the grown-ups the way to go forward," she said.

Jella thought she saw more than one shrug of a "star-studded shoulder," but no one spoke until General McClure stood up. He didn't pooh-pooh her proposal but, in proper army fashion, asked where the money for such an exhibit was to come from. The budget provided nothing for children's books.

"General, if I may ask," she replied, "why did headquarters take on an adviser for women's and youth affairs if there were no means to implement the position?"

Everyone, including the general, smiled.

"That's not a bad point," he said, but he didn't know where they could find the money. It was, however, General McClure thought, an excellent plan. He'd send a memo to Washington, DC.

Jella was quite sure that memos to Washington, even if successful, would take months to implement. She couldn't wait for the American government to act. It was up to her.

She asked the general for permission to get the books without any money. Books that didn't cost anything? That idea was much more appealing to the big brass. General McClure was very pleased, but he did remind her that up until a few months before, most of the world considered Germany their enemy. Were they really going to be sending her crates of books for nothing?

Jella herself felt a twinge of doubt, but she suppressed it. "If the war really is over—if one is to believe in peaceful coexistence—the first messengers of that peace will be these children's books," she said. "Help me with this experiment. I promise you'll never regret it."

The general promised to back the project not only by sending the memo but also by noting in writing that the "International Exhibition of Children's Books," as he named it, would have top priority.

She didn't hug the general, but she wanted to.

Now to get the books. Dozens of letters would have to be written and sent. There was, of course, no internet or email in those days, and access to a typewriter was heavily monitored. Jella would steal into the typewriter room after working hours and try to type quietly, but inevitably one of the guards would come by and ask her what she was doing there. She was afraid to say that she was writing requests for children's books. What soldier would accept such a reason? So she would simply mumble some high-ranking officer's name as though she had been cruelly ordered to do his work late into the night. Jella never seemed to mind a bit of subterfuge in pursuit of her goals.

The letters pleaded for books, especially picture books, to show the children of Germany what the free world was like. They would be part of an international exhibition of children's books and serve as messengers of peace. German publishers might decide to translate and publish many of them.

The letters also asked for paintings and drawings done by the children of the
country. German children would understand this universal language and be cheered
by it. With the help of friends who had diplomatic connections, Jella sent letters to
publishers in 20 countries. Then the waiting began.

Postal service in war-torn Europe was slow and undependable. But at last the first reply arrived. The French would take part! Norway, which had suffered so much under Nazi occupation, replied sadly that there were no books readily available, but they had asked Norwegian children to look through their own shelves and send along any books they might want to share with the children of Germany. Denmark and the Netherlands sent similar replies. The neutral nations Sweden and Switzerland joined the effort, as did the United States.

Of the 20 letters Jella sent, only one came back with a no. The Belgians apologized but could not see themselves sending symbols of goodwill to a country that had invaded them not once but twice in less than 25 years. Undaunted, Jella wrote back to remind them that children had not been a part of those wars. This was Belgium's chance to win the German children over so that they would not suffer a third invasion. Even the reluctant publishers saw the logic of this appeal and joined the effort.

Early that spring, Jella met someone who was to become a friend and ally in her efforts: She was invited back to Frankfurt to meet Eleanor Roosevelt, who was on her own fact-finding trip to war-torn Europe. Jella was able to tell the former first lady of the United States about the coming exhibition and about her dream of making peace through children's books. Mrs. Roosevelt promised her assistance, and in time she would prove to be a tremendous help.

The official approval for the exhibition would come on March 29, 1946, but Jella needed to act sooner. The books would be arriving, and an exhibit hall had to be located. One of the few suitable venues left undamaged was in the city of Munich, long a center of the arts. In 1933 the Nazis had built a huge museum there, calling it the Haus der Kunst, or House of Art. Built to hold "true" German art, as opposed to the modern art that the Nazis considered "degenerate," it was a monumentally ugly building, nicknamed by locals "Hitler's Bavarian Sausage Factory." It seemed ironic

that it should survive destruction when so many older and more beautiful buildings had been destroyed. The occupying Americans had taken over one of the largest rooms for an officers' mess. But beyond the dining hall, room after room was empty except for all the symbols of Nazism that decorated the walls.

Jella formed a committee of local German citizens and their occupiers to ready the rooms for the many books she knew would be on the way. American, French, and British forces all helped with needed supplies, but the committee did the hammering, scrubbing, and painting. One day Jella came upon a professor who was passionately painting over a swastika. "We should be chiseling it out," he said, "not painting it over."

The first crates of books began to arrive. It was an exciting moment. But perhaps more significant to Jella were the children's paintings. American children, who had never known bombs or heard the boots of an invading enemy, painted in bold colors huge, happy pictures of the lives and places they knew. English children painted the guards outside Buckingham Palace, big portraits of Churchill, the fishing boats at Dunkirk, and always the British Royal Air Force planes in the sky. Swedish children chose to portray ships going out to sea with red-nosed and rosy-cheeked captains at the helm. Pictures from France and Switzerland were mostly in pastel colors, showing peaceful rural scenes, although one French child had drawn a bazooka peeking out a window. Saddest of all was work by German children, which Jella had also collected—cramped, gritty pictures covered every inch of the paper, depicting ruin after ruin. Though, occasionally, a young German artist would retreat into fantasy with Cinderella at the ball or the dream image of a huge loaf of bread.

Opening day was set for July 5, 1946. The books were all on display. The pictures were hung. The long-awaited exhibit was ready for the public.

The military authorities had arranged for really important guests to preview the exhibition. Although Jella couldn't help but fret about the response of these VIPs, she needn't have worried. Erich Kästner, the author of the favorite German children's book *Emil and the Detectives*, covered the event for the American German-language newspaper. Most of Kästner's books had been burned by the Nazis, but somehow Emil and his clever friends had survived destruction. The book was too popular, or perhaps the Nazis felt it was harmless. Who would believe a gang of kids could capture a crook who had outwitted the police in several cities?

Kästner didn't report on any of the long-winded speeches or bother to name-drop the noted invitees. For him the distinguished guests were the characters, both human and animal, from the books on display. "Space does not permit me to give the full names and birthplaces of all the princes, kings, fairies, charcoal burners, pirates, witches, captains, heroes, and magicians who attended the opening, but maybe this summary recalls a lot of them to mind. Whosoever wishes to pay them a visit may do so. Their address is: Haus der Kunst, Munich, Germany. Open daily from 9 to 11 a.m., and from 2 to 5 p.m. Come as you are. Adults may tag along, too."

And they came. Just as they were, with their ragged clothes, dirty shoes, and eager faces. Every morning, long before nine, the line began forming, waiting for entry. There were some families in the queue, especially on Sundays, but more often it was children on their own. Stern adults had warned that these ragamuffins would destroy the books—perhaps the hall itself. But they never did. And although these were mostly children who were hungry for books, hardly any went missing.

In Munich, Jella had
been fortunate enough to find
a hall undamaged by the war,

but she wanted the exhibit to move so
that more people, especially children,
could see the books and pictures. In her
own inimitable way, she made it happen.

In Stuttgart, Frankfurt, and Württemberg, she sought out libraries or museums that
could be brought back from ruin. Without bothering with official memos or written
authorizations, she simply invoked the magic words *American authorities* to get
access and needed materials for renovation.

Invariably children handled the precious books with care. In every city, the exhibit was truly nourishment for hungry spirits. And in each place the exhibition visited, the children begged to take the books home. But Jella always had to refuse. The books had other cities to visit, and when their journey was over, she dreamed she might find a permanent home for them.

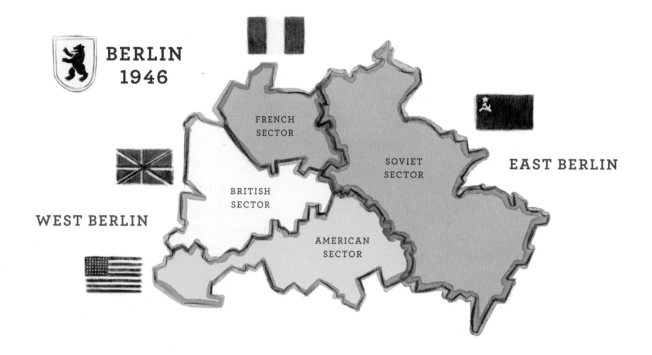

The last stop for the exhibition was the US Information Center in West Berlin. West Berliners, surrounded as they were by the Russian occupation zone, were thrilled with this visit from the free outside world. But they were worried. Would everyone, including former Nazis, be admitted? Of course everyone would be welcome, Jella said. She knew it would not be wise to ask questions about anyone's past.

Opening day in Berlin was December 6, 1946. Jella said the best opening speech was given by a little girl who, when she spied Santa Claus and his reindeer decorating the wall, exclaimed, "Oh, now it is peace. Yes, now it is peace."

The plight of Berlin's children that cold December seemed particularly bleak. Since it was nearly Christmas, wouldn't it be wonderful if Jella could give them each the gift of a book of their own? One night, sitting on the steps of the US Information Center, she reread *The Story of Ferdinand* by her friend Munro Leaf. Jella decided on the spot that she simply had to give the story of the gentle bull to the children of Berlin. She translated it into German, and then, as she had many times before, she enlisted the allies she needed—influential citizens, the American government, and a local newspaper that had plenty of newsprint. The newspaper printed 50,000 copies of Jella's translation of Leaf's story with Robert Lawson's pictures and folded each into a little book. Just before Christmas, Jella stood at the entrance of the exhibit and passed out copies of *The Story of Ferdinand* to every child who came in.

"What did you do about copyright?" she was asked by a publisher sometime
later. She told the inquirer, a bit cavalierly, that she just forgot about copyright. But one
had to believe that even if they weren't consulted beforehand, Munro Leaf and Robert
Lawson, knowing the joy their work had brought to hungry children, would, in the spirit
of Ferdinand, find a way to forgive her.

Jella arranged two other Christmas gifts for the children of Germany.

Her friend Erich Kästner translated Clement Clarke Moore's poem "A Visit from St. Nicholas" (perhaps better known as "'Twas the Night Before Christmas"), and Emery Condor drew illustrations.

The US Army–run tabloid newspaper *Heute*, or *Today*, where Jella had recently been appointed managing editor, published the poem and turned it, like *The Story of Ferdinand*, into a little folded book dedicated to the children of Germany.

German children had heard rumors of the Walt Disney film *Snow White and the Seven Dwarfs*. Although already released in 1937 and shown all over the world,

no
one
had seen
it in Germany.
Disagreements
between the American
and German film companies
had, as Jella said, kept Snow
White in her glass coffin with no
Prince Charming to rescue her. Jella
may not have been Prince Charming,
but when she wanted something for
the children, she found a way. She
wrote directly to Walt Disney
and asked him to allow
Christmastime showings for
the children of Germany.
Disney relented for the
season, then, as Jella
tells it, Snow White
was put back to
rest in her
glass
coffin.

At the end of 1946, Jella was summoned to Munich. There were two newspapers published for the German people by the American authorities: *Heute* and *Die Neue Zeitung* (The New Times). Both were housed in the former building for the *Völkischer Beobachter* (People's Observer)—the official newspaper of the Nazi party. Hitler had bought the paper in 1921, and by 1944 it had a circulation of 1.7 million.

The Americans had taken over the building and the printing presses, but Jella could still imagine the sound of goose-stepping Nazis echoing through the halls and stairways.

The staffs of the newspapers, however, were composed of top-notch journalists and photographers. Not all the staff had the same respect for children that Jella had. When, one Christmas, *Heute* proposed to use as its cover a picture drawn by a child, one of the Americans cried, "Over my dead body!" and suggested instead a picture of a Christmas cover girl. But as usual, Jella found a way to prevail. The child's painting of a Christmas celebration in a snow-covered village was chosen, along with a poem:

> *Stop telling us of war and destruction,*
> *The children cry out*
> *Across the boundaries*
> *That adults establish.*
> *And they press gloriously on*
> *Into the uncharted future,*
> *Creating again what the other*
> *So mercilessly ruined.*

One sleepless night, Jella got the idea for a collection of bedtime stories for children. The newspaper would solicit the public for submissions and print the best ones.

Submissions came pouring in—20,000 or so. Almost all of the stories were horribly sentimental, telling of little snowflakes or wee dewdrops or tiny roses. Not one hinted that the events of the last 20 years had ever happened—and this was a country famous for the very unsentimental tales of wolves and witches collected by the Brothers Grimm. Finally they were able to find enough good stories to publish in the paper and eventually collect in a book.

But the finest story that came out of that time was one that Jella and her friend Erich Kästner came up with. Jella kept thinking about all the international conferences going on in the immediate postwar period and the fact that they all seemed to come to nothing. Their failure was sure to result in the deaths and suffering of children in still more wars. Maybe the future of the world should be turned over to the animals. She went to Kästner with the idea.

Was she thinking about a book for adults?

"Yes and no," Jella said. "I think it would have to address itself beyond children to adults."

And so Kästner—with his wife at his side and his cat, Mickey, riding his shoulder—would come every evening to Jella's apartment to work on the project.

"I see Mickey came along, too," Jella once said, trying to pet the cat, which hissed at her in return.

"He's got the leading role," Kästner said. "How can we write about a conference run by animals without any animals?"

Kästner's *The Animals' Conference* was eventually published with illustrations by Walter Trier. With great humor it tells how animals from elephants to polar bears band together in a mighty campaign to force generals and politicians to make peace for the sake of the children of the world.

Kästner wasn't sure a book for children would appeal to adults. But Jella argued that war touched everyone. She recalled her trip to the Berchtesgadener Hof in the Bavarian Alps a few years ago. It had been a fancy resort hotel before the Nazis took it over, and then a favorite retreat of the Nazi high command. During the occupation, it was a retreat for top American officers. In the summer of 1946, a high-ranking general had invited Jella to visit. The idea of vacationing in one of Hitler's favorite spots was sickening. But for someone in the army, a general's invitation is akin to a command, so she went.

She was shown to a beautiful room with a breathtaking view of the Alps. When the maid appeared and discovered that Jella spoke German, she was delighted: "Oh, Madam, nobody around here speaks anything but English. It was altogether different before. Der Führer [Hitler] used to stay here, [Hermann] Göring, [Joseph] Goebbels . . . Oh, those were the days."

Jella felt compelled to give the poor maid a history lesson, but it fell on deaf ears. "Oh," she said, "you didn't know those gentlemen, Madam. People have given you a false picture of them."

No, Nazism had not died with the death of Hitler.

Ever since she had been assigned to Munich, Jella had been wondering how the traveling show could be turned into a real library: the International Youth Library, as she called her dream. And she wasn't the only dreamer. Her desk drawers were full of letters requesting that she find a permanent home for the precious books.

She pushed her plan for a library so hard and so frequently that she could see the alarm on officers' faces when they saw her coming. But what was she to do about money? She had proved that she could get free books, but a free building to house them in and salaries for staff and funds for maintenance? That was another story.

Then one day she was told she had visitors. Two gentlemen in civilian dress were ushered into her office. They had seen the exhibition in Berlin and had been very impressed by it. They were representatives from the Rockefeller Foundation. "The idea of international understanding through books for children and young people interests us," they said. "Tell us more about it."

Jella poured out her dreams to them. They said, "Maybe we'll be able to help you somewhat. Send us a detailed plan for this International Youth Library." They promised Jella she would hear from them again.

The representatives from the Rockefeller Foundation were as good as their word. A letter came inviting Jella to come to the United States for a lecture tour. For several months she was to speak on promoting international understanding through children's books.

Upon Jella's departure in April 1948, a German reporter asked if she'd be traveling alone. "Indeed not," she answered. "Thousands of children hungry for books are flying along with me."

After the rubble-strewn cities of England and Germany, the shining skyscrapers of New York City were a startling sight. Her first stop was Rockefeller Center to get her touring schedule. The view from the building's windows was breathtaking. Jella was scheduled to appear at almost every book-related event in the next few months, meeting teachers, librarians, publishers, and leaders of youth organizations. It would be her job to find a sponsor for her dream library and millionaires who might contribute to it. She was to collect books, records, children's paintings, films—all as gifts, of course. There was, as usual, no money for purchases.

Her next visit was to her old friend General McClure in his New York field office. He'd already seen her garner hundreds of books for the price of 20 postage stamps. "How many crates should I expect to have ready to ship your booty home?" he asked. He may have been joking, but Jella did want to fill many crates on this trip.

She addressed both the Association for Childhood Education International and the American Library Association, telling them of her dream of an international library of children's books. "What can we do to help?" was the response she heard everywhere. At the University of Chicago, someone objected not to a library but to the fact that Jella was asking that it be located in Germany. Why Germany, after all the suffering that Germany had caused the world?

"Even if your prejudices are partly justified, please try to overcome them," she said to the unhappy audience. "The most important thing is to give the children of Germany a chance."

Jella won over the crowd, and in the end, the University of Chicago formed a committee of support that would make valuable contributions to the library.

There was even a delightful visit to the Pentagon, where Jella was reunited with old friends from the occupation. Everyone seemed to be having a good time. After all, as Jella has said, even generals were once children. She overheard two officers reciting nursery rhymes to each other across their desks. But it wasn't just playtime. Jella and the Pentagon officers spent time drawing up strategic plans, not for how to wage a war but for how to wage peace. Erich Kästner's animals would have been very pleased.

On her second trip to New York, Jella visited the Museum of Modern Art. It was not the paintings of modern masters that impressed her most, but the art classes for children. Three- and four-year-olds stood happily working away,

smearing bright colors across large expanses of newsprint and their own clothes and faces with no adult trying to correct them or instruct them. Her library would have a space like that, she decided—a place where children could paint what they wished, how they wished. She must have remembered the sad, cramped pictures German children had contributed to the exhibition. That would change in her dream library.

In the New York Public Library, she got another idea for the one she hoped to build. It welcomed immigrant and refugee children not only with a restful space but also with books in the languages of their homelands. Yes, her library would welcome all those ragged refugee children by sharing with them books in their own languages.

Eleanor Roosevelt invited Jella for dinner at her New York apartment and the next day wrote about Jella in her column, "My Day," which was read by millions of Americans. "Yes," she wrote, "the time has come to help the German children as well as the other children of Europe. But don't forget to send books as well as food. We must not let the children grow up again into young Nazis and Fascists, so we have to give them food for thought." Offers of help began pouring in from readers. Reporters called for interviews. General McClure's crates wouldn't remain empty.

Mrs. Roosevelt also cabled her friend General Lucius D. Clay in Berlin asking him to help, and the general wired right back assuring Mrs. Roosevelt and Jella that he would.

Upon leaving the wealth of America behind, it was a shock to return to Munich, where the American army was crying poor. Reform of the currency had gone into effect. The army now had no extra funds to spend on a library for children's books. But Eleanor Roosevelt's cable to General Clay had worked its magic. Somehow, as tight as budgets were, Jella was allowed to go ahead with her project. She was given two tiny rooms in the courthouse of the American forces. Often she would spy handcuffed prisoners being escorted past her door. A lot of proposed projects had been axed, and there was a stream of messages warning

that her secretary and handyman were to be fired. Jella had to go to the personnel office and plead that without her tiny staff, she could not do the job that the commanding general was backing, before the threats of firing were rescinded.

But there was no possibility of starting her library in two tiny rooms. She had to find not only a home for the precious collection but also space for all the children who would crowd into it every day. She drove all over the ruins of Munich looking for the perfect building. Then one day she came upon a house that, though damaged, was still standing, and, as she said, she "fell head over heels in love." She didn't know who owned it or, indeed, if anyone was living in it, but in true Jella fashion, she set out to acquire it.

Bureaucracy is a problem in any country, but in occupied Germany, Jella had to deal with both the occupation forces and the local German authorities. That the owner of the house was the Bavarian Ministry of Culture didn't make negotiations any simpler. The ministry didn't even know that a cosmetics manufacturer, the Institute of Beauty, was squatting in the basement and not eager to move out. Even when the Americans gave the factory space in an old barracks, the Ministry of Culture still dragged its feet.

Alois Hundhammer, a minister who had been so outspokenly anti-Nazi that he had been forced to spend time in a concentration camp, said a firm no. He felt that there were too many far more pressing needs than a children's library. Jella wouldn't back down, and their arguments became so heated that the man's poor assistant often felt the need to intervene. One day Jella was ready to storm out of a fiery session, when she cried, "Generations of children will curse you if you keep us from building [the] International Youth Library!"

She saw Herr Hundhammer's face grow pale and realized she'd gone too far. She calmed herself down and went back to offer him her hand in apology. He took it. The next day she received a letter giving her permission to use the building.

By 1948 tensions between the Soviet Union and the West had grown to the point that the American military was giving its civilians directions on what to do in the case of an "uprising." Of course, it was not a revolt of the German citizenry that was feared, but another, far worse world war. Meanwhile, in Germany Jella could see that the denazification of the adult population was less than complete. Judges and professionals of every kind who had certainly been Nazi sympathizers seemed to be quietly resuming their former places of authority.

So the children somehow had to be saved, or they would be at the mercy of this untrustworthy and warring adult world. It would take time to make the building habitable. She urged the workers to hurry—though, she said, there was no need for her urging. The workers were her allies, and she had another unexpected ally in Franz Stadelmayer, the acting mayor of Munich. Although he said he knew nothing about children's books other than the ones he'd read as a boy, he joined the cause and founded the Society of Friends of the International Youth Library, enlisting prominent German citizens as the first members. Such an organization was a requirement for a grant from the Rockefeller Foundation.

So her plans were going forward. She had the eager cooperation of the workers restoring the damaged building, and American and German authorities were lending their support.

She even had a new office, moving from a virtual jailhouse to an actual palace. The Prinz Carl Palais was huge. Why not invite children to come in for story time?

Count Clemens Graf von Podewils, the caretaker, refused. *Their dirty shoes would mar the gorgeous floors*, he argued. They could leave their shoes at the door, Jella replied. *But they would run and send the ancient Greek vases crashing.* Just lock the vases up. *Locked doors prove irresistible to street urchins.* Jella wore down the count's objections. The banquet hall was opened to the children. No floors were scuffed, and no vases smashed.

In the spring of 1949, Jella received the cable she had been waiting for:
ROCKEFELLER FOUNDATION APPROVES A TWO-YEAR GRANT OF $22,000 FOR
THE ESTABLISHMENT OF AN INTERNATIONAL YOUTH LIBRARY. She had the
backing of Eleanor Roosevelt and, thanks to her, General Lucius D. Clay. There was no
stopping her now. The dream of the International Youth Library would become a reality.

The opening day festivities, on September 14, 1949, had the usual speeches from officials and VIPs, but for Jella and perhaps many in the audience, the most important part of the ceremony was the part played by children. The young readers chose their favorite books from the collection and read them in their original languages. An American boy read *The Story of Ferdinand*; the young reader of *The Wonderful Adventures of Nils* was Swedish; an Italian child read *The Adventures of Pinocchio*; a Swiss girl read *Heidi*; a German boy read *Emil and the Detectives*; a French child read *The Story of Babar: The Little Elephant*. The program of children reading, singing, and dancing was broadcast internationally by radio.

While children flocked to the library, severe German librarians lamented that the books were being handled by children who had no soap and, even worse, that the collection had not been cataloged in the proper German manner—or, for that matter, cataloged at all.

Predictions about the library's future were dire, the worst being that the children would steal all the books. But they didn't. The children relished the fact that their library's books had been sent from friends overseas. They monitored each other for dirty fingernails and runny noses. Most accepted the fact that this was a reference library only, but if a child couldn't resist borrowing a book to take home, there was a special shelf to which it could be quietly returned—no questions asked.

Since there was no other library quite like it, the original "cataloging" was by language, then by subject. Eventually, the American Library Association was asked to send an expert to sort out this informal system into something more professionally acceptable.

But the lack of proper cataloging was not something that disturbed the young patrons. They loved every aspect of the library, from the art studio where they could paint whatever and however they wished to the story hour. But perhaps most exciting was the privilege of going to the shelf and picking out one's own book. The children were urged to write reviews of books they had read.

"Tell me," a university professor from America asked Jella, "how can Nazi parents give birth to children such as these?"

"The fact," Jella replied, "is that every child is the start of a new life. That's the whole secret."

Book discussion groups were organized, with publishers donating sets of paperback books that the participants could read, either singly or as a group, and then discuss. A radio station heard of this project and asked if they could tape these conversations for later broadcast. Jella was apprehensive about this. She wanted the participants to enjoy the freewheeling discussions, not groom themselves to become radio stars, but she relented, hoping the broadcasts would encourage more widespread support for the library.

Once, when a book about refugees was to be discussed, the German author and her publisher were invited to attend. A young person briefly presented the book's contents and themes, but the children wanted to question the visiting author.

They demanded to know if she was a refugee. She wasn't. The many children in the group who were refugees gave her a list of errors they'd found in her book. That was painful enough, but the worst question was still to come:

"Did you ever think of why there are refugees? Or whose fault it is?" the child asked, and then answered his own question.

"It's your Hitler's fault, the man you broke into wild rhapsodies about in the children's books you wrote during the war." And these children had done their research. They quoted passages from the author's wartime books back to her.

Jella wasn't quite sure what to do. The mic was live. The poor writer was close to tears. "I fell victim to Hitler through false idealism," she said. "Don't you allow people to see their errors and change?"

"Yes," was the reply, "when the change is genuine. But we can't allow them to write books for us so soon again."

The station broadcast this discussion unedited, but there was more difficulty with a later discussion, when the children took on their own parents.

The book was one that supported parental authority as absolute.

"Never. Our parents have left us with a horrible legacy, and we no longer believe [they] are infallible."

The youngest member of the group cried out, "Parents should be done away with altogether!"

Everyone burst out laughing at the absurdity of the suggestion, but that didn't keep the radio station executives from summoning Jella into their offices. "We'll have to delete that part," they said.

"Delete it? Why?" Jella asked, playing innocent. "People can speak freely in Germany now."

And somehow free speech won, and the cry to eliminate parents, along with the laughter, went out over the airwaves.

The ever-helpful Erich Kästner led a playwrights' group, though perhaps *refereed* would be a better word than *led*. Although the decision had been made to write a play together, there was heated disagreement as to what the play should be about. Some young would-be playwrights demanded that it be about real life, while others wanted something more fantastic.

"What about a fairy tale?" one of the younger members of the group suggested, only to be pounced upon and told to return to the nursery where he obviously belonged.

Kästner stepped in. Why couldn't it be a combination of ideas? Couldn't they meet somehow in the middle? So the proposed drama became *Our Search for Fairy Tales in the Big City*.

And, because no one wanted to play a minor role in the upcoming production, they decided to write the play with 15 major roles—one for each participant. There is no known record of the script or the production. Perhaps that is just as well.

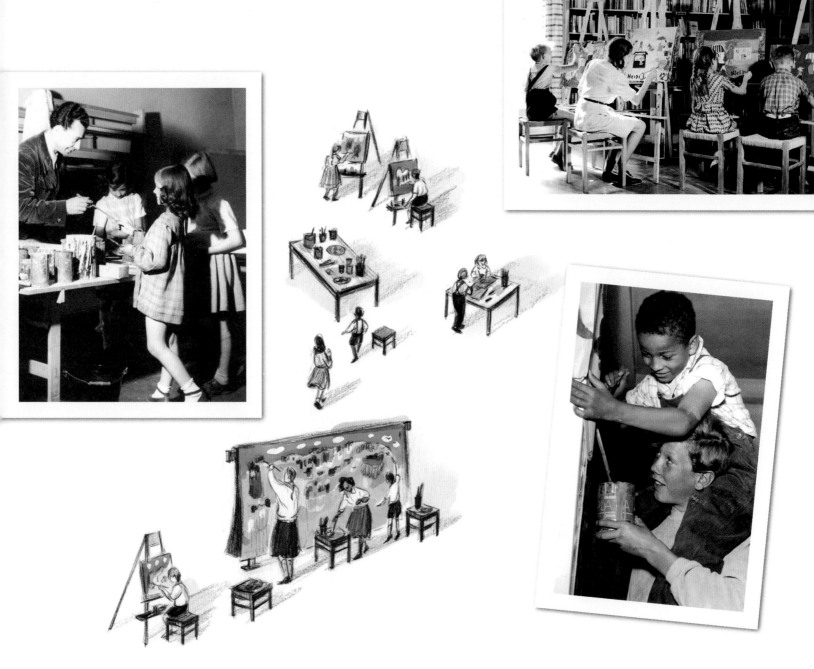

The art studio was a favorite place for children but a source of consternation for proper German librarians and academics. It was presided over by Ferdinand Steidle, an artist in his own right. He would begin a session with a fairy tale, a Bible story, or perhaps a scene from the everyday life of a child. The story was meant, of course, to inspire the artwork, but the children would question and argue and often adapt or reject the prompt altogether as they grabbed their donated brushes and watercolors and went to work furiously on their pieces of newsprint or brown wrapping paper. When Steidle asked one little painter about a strange fuzzy creature clinging to Noah's robe, the child answered, "That's my dog, Asso."

Never content to confine her efforts to Germany, Jella decided to have an exhibition of international children's self-portraits. The collected paintings were first shown in Germany but eventually toured a number of countries. Columbia University asked for a second showing in New York City. They wanted to study the portraits to see what they revealed.

Nevertheless, the art studio continued to be attacked by Germany's "experts" and government bureaucrats. What did painting have to do with libraries? No money would be put into the budget for that! Jella, of course, found a way around that as well, and it seems that no one quite dared to challenge her rearrangement of funds.

For parents who didn't want their children to waste time at the library, Jella promoted the idea of learning a foreign language—French, Italian, Spanish, English—through children's books. Again the experts were skeptical, but the children loved the method, and their understanding of other languages flourished. It was much more fun to learn a language through a story than through a sterile textbook.

The children were learning about other children around the world, looking at their self-portraits, reading the same books. *Why not,* thought Jella, *host a Children's United Nations (UN)?* But not "children's," the young people said. "We're no longer children. The war made us grow up fast."

"I tramped from Dresden to Nuremberg with only my two little sisters, and I was so intent on getting away that I forgot my sixth birthday," said one.

"I was jailed in my village for just stealing a loaf of bread," said another.

"When bomb splinters hit my mother, I had to make an emergency dressing for her with my handkerchief, or otherwise she would have bled to death. I was seven then."

No, these children had missed out on childhood, and there was no going back. Their organization would be the Young People's United Nations.

Another challenge emerged with the choosing of delegates to represent the 60 countries in the actual UN. Germany, at that time, only had an observer in the UN, but in the youth version, it would be allowed a delegation. There was fierce competition for the more popular countries like the United States, England, Sweden, and the Netherlands. Some of the other delegations were a bit harder to fill. One shy child agreed to take Russia—not the Soviet Union, he insisted, just Russia. The next task was to research the chosen countries so the delegates could properly represent them. The delegates visited consulates, travel bureaus, airline offices, museums, and libraries.

The discussions at the flag-laden tables in the art studio were intense. Were armies needed to ensure world peace? They voted for a United Nations Peace Force.

They were against racial segregation and castigated the US delegation for its nation's failures.

Although the delegates tended to disdain politics, the young people knew the UN demanded their involvement and so proclaimed, "Politics, yes. Party politics, no."

Meanwhile, the United Nations meeting in New York drafted a children's charter, "The Declaration of the Rights of the Child." It was to ensure "the normal and healthy development of every child in freedom and dignity." Since it was in draft form, the young people felt they should make suggestions for its improvement.

The charter expressed concern for orphans. How about children from broken homes? Didn't they deserve concern?

There was nothing forbidding the conscription of child soldiers. Delegates told their stories of being in the Hitler Youth and the Werewolf troops. A child refugee from Korea declared that child conscription was still occurring, that it happened in Korea every day.

Jella made sure that the minutes of the session along with the delegates' suggestions for improving the charter were sent to New York. Sadly there was no response from the "adult" UN, but the United Nations Educational, Scientific and Cultural Organization (UNESCO) eventually paid a goodwill visit to a Young People's UN session, and the International Youth Library (IYL) was designated as an associated project of UNESCO.

Jella was never idle. Perhaps harking back to her teenage years, when she established a library for immigrant workers' children in Stuttgart, she began a campaign to establish libraries in German factories with, of course, children's book sections. Her idea was to ship crates of books through the International Youth Library. In addition, it would help train company librarians and provide booklists and tours of the IYL, which would serve as a model library. Unfortunately, Jella was not able to offer funds for these projects, and her entreaties to wealthy German industrialists fell on deaf ears. These powerful men lacked the vision of the Rockefeller Foundation. Children's books did not have the same allure as a plaque in a museum or art gallery in thanks for a valuable gift.

But on to perhaps her greatest achievement: Jella had been seeking to make peace through children's books since 1949. Perhaps she should gather people from around the world who also gave their lives to children and their books, who might also believe that books could be a bridge for peace. Jella made up a list of people she considered the who's who of children's literature and sent out 60 invitations. Very quickly the acceptances poured in, along with pleas from people who had not received an invitation but who wanted to come.

Jella had assembled an impressive list of participants, so she was determined to get an outstanding keynote speaker. The famous Spanish philosopher José Ortega y Gasset was currently a guest lecturer at the University of Munich. Jella wrote Ortega y Gasset but got no reply. One day she was having lunch at a favorite restaurant. It was crowded, and a gentleman asked if he could share her table. It was the professor himself.

Jella introduced herself and told him that her guardian angel must have arranged the meeting. The dismayed man apologized for not replying but said that he was only in Munich for his work at the university.

But, said Jella, how could he argue with the angel who had brought them together?

He couldn't. Ortega y Gasset's speech about the importance of childhood and the need to preserve the child within inspired the conference goers. And before they went home, on November 18, 1951, they voted to establish the International Board on Books for Young People (IBBY, the acronym by which the organization is known even today).

Switzerland, whose people had not been to war since 1847, was to be the home of the new organization. The first official meeting was held in Zurich at the Federal Institute of Technology. Two hundred participants attended, discussing everything from the value of comic books to the establishment of an international prize for children's literature to be named for Hans Christian Andersen. IBBY decided to include an honors list of the best books from all the participating countries.

Jella found children's literature experts easier to deal with than German bureaucrats. Since the government in Bonn had become the chief funding source for the youth library, Jella was now forced to sit down with officials who did not understand or share her original dream. The library collection should be a place for scholarly research and for publishers to see the latest books from abroad, they said. What place did children have in such a library? They saw no reason for book discussion groups, language classes, or a Young People's UN, and certainly not for an art studio.

Jella never stopped dreaming—or fighting. She had often spoken to people in America about her wish to have a bookmobile, like the ones she had seen in her American travels. In 1956 a generous friend in Texas donated money for the vehicle. When Jella announced this great news to the board in Munich, a cry went up. What about the cost of gas? What about the cost of another librarian, not to mention the purchase of books for the project? They wanted to return the money, but that seemed impractical because it might cause diplomatic hard feelings. Fortunately, someone at UNESCO provided a discreet solution: The bookmobile would be transported to another country that could put it to proper use!

In 1957 Jella retired from the library built by her dreams and fierce determination. Her vision for the library was too far removed from that of the bureaucrats who controlled most of the funding. She moved to Zurich and would no longer be expending time and energy battling or skirting around petty officials or military brass to translate her dreams into reality.

In 1961 she was able to carry out a mission first proposed by friends from the Rockefeller Foundation. In a joint project with UNESCO, Jella was asked to visit countries in the Middle East, promoting children's books as an instrument for cultivating world peace. She could hardly have dreamed up a more ideal assignment for herself.

This time, instead of collecting
books, she would be sending crates of books
to give away. Unfortunately, most of the book crates
disappeared en route or were confiscated for vague
bureaucratic reasons. But she herself traveled safely, and with her went
her lifetime joy of reading and sharing books with children.

The journey began with a stop in New York, where she saw friends at the
Rockefeller Foundation and the New York Public Library. She even made a trip to
the Pentagon and reconnected with American officers who had made the first book
exhibitions possible. After a few more stops in the States, she was off to the Middle
East: Istanbul, in Turkey; Tehran, in Iran; and Beirut, in Lebanon. She was making
these trips in comfortable airplane seats, not strapped to the metal bucket seat of a
military transport.

Back home in Zurich, she wrote about this trip in her memoir, *A Bridge of Children's Books*, which begins with her conversation with the rude colonel sitting next to her on the flight to Frankfurt in 1945.

Letters she wrote to her son, Gunther, during her years of "retirement" in Zurich reveal that Jella never really retired. She was in demand as a speaker and translator. Friends from around the world came calling, and she was a part of a lively social group.

She maintained her connection to IBBY, and those who remember her with great admiration also allowed quietly that she could sometimes be difficult to work with. Jella herself cheerfully confessed how she confronted military protocol and local officials with fierce resistance and shameless wiles, so it is little wonder that working with her proved challenging. Perhaps all accomplished women throughout history have at some point in their lives been labeled "difficult to work with."

But this formidable woman had a warm side, which she revealed in letters to her son during her final years. Her love for her two children, who as teenagers had fled Nazi Germany with her in 1936, and for their families is evident. Her daughter-in-law, whom she had openly disapproved of in earlier years, is kindly addressed with questions about her health and well-being. In one letter, she speaks glowingly of her granddaughter, Claudia. Claudia had thought Jella disapproved of her as well, but in this letter, Jella calls her "a wonderful child" and remarks on how intelligent and well-mannered she was.

Claudia recalls how Jella would send her books and how, after receiving one of the obligatory thank you notes, Jella wrote back to tell Claudia that she should consider becoming a writer. Jella would surely be pleased to know that she has.

The final letter in the collection kept by her son is dated August 12, 1970. Jella exults in the family reunion at Suisi, a beautiful resort in the Swiss Alps, and expresses her deep love and concern for all the family. She also raves about Claudia. But then, the woman who seemed never to flag says that upon her arrival home in Zurich, "I was tired beyond word and am afraid [I] still am." She died in Zurich on the morning of October 4, 1970. But her dreams live on.

In 1983 the International Youth Library moved from the house Jella had found for it in 1949 to the Blutenburg Castle, a gorgeous medieval building that is called, appropriately, the Book Castle.

Today it houses more than 600,000 items, the largest collection of children's and youth books

in the world, and conducts countless exhibitions and activities centered on children's books and their authors and illustrators. But just as important, it is the vibrant home of Jella Lepman's lifelong dream . . . and of the dreams of generations of children who have found hope and solace in the pages of a book.

IBBY headquarters are now in Basel, Switzerland, reaching out to 80 member nations with the message that children's books are a bridge to peace. Germany is now a prosperous and unified nation, but elsewhere in the world there are many children who are cold, hungry, and homeless—children who suffer because of war and natural disasters. IBBY representatives are working on their behalf in many of these places. And all these children, like the children in a devastated Germany of 1945, need books to nourish their minds and spirits.

Every two years, IBBY members meet in a world congress. They have met on every continent except Antarctica to talk about books and the children who need them. Strapped into her bucket seat beside the American colonel, Jella Lepman, for all her imagination, could not have dreamed what her return to Germany in 1945 would mean for the children of the world.

Acknowledgments

We gratefully acknowledge the remarkable, dedicated, and tenacious work of the International Youth Library (IYL, www.ijb.de), Munich; its director, Dr. Christiane Raabe, and executive assistant, Rebecca Wilhelm, without whose support, cooperation, and help this book could never have seen the light of day; and Claudia Lepman Logan, who provided the author with invaluable and previously unpublished information about her grandmother.

The photographs in this book were drawn from an exquisite recent German edition of Jella Lepman's memoir, *Die Kinderbuchbrücke* (A Bridge of Children's Books) (Verlag Antje Kunstmann, 2020), produced by the IYL in collaboration with the Lepman scholar Anna Becchi. The memoir contains valuable supplementary material, including an insightful biographical profile by Becchi that was most helpful in the preparation of this text.

Photo Credits

The International Youth Library
Schloss Blutenburg (Blutenburg Castle)
Munich, Germany

THE LIBRARY (AND CASTLE!) ENTRANCE

A STORY CIRCLE

A WORKSHOP IN THE LIBRARY

THE CHAMBER OF LITERARY TREASURES

CHILDREN EXPLORING AN EXHIBITION

THE UNDERGROUND STACKS